Pondering Eros

a compilation of feminine & erotic poetics

Bridget Crown

BookLeaf
Publishing

India | USA | UK

Made with ❤ on the BookLeaf Publishing Platform
www.bookleafpub.in
www.bookleafpub.com

Dedication

*dedicated to all lovers
and those willing to fight for love*

Preface

I began by looking at the erotic as an energy exchange that takes place apart from the body, to have these as necessary soul experiences that give way to an understanding of ones self in a larger context. Sensuality through erotic experiences has taught me about gender, about loving, about further reaching truths having to do with a largely non verbal yet highly communicative practice. Just as love is a practice, skill, and karmic art form, a successful exploration of pleasure lends itself to relational qualities like humility and obstacles having to do with understanding that each of us must face with empathy in order to give and receive with comfort within the context of intimacy.

Acknowledgements

Those who have taught me about love, those who have held me accountable, and those who live authentically everyday.

1. vanity

squishing, scrubbing, obsessing
skin, face, eyes,
checking and double checking,
icing and reddening,

smooth, heaven sent, radiant,
smile, teeth white, head tilted back,
the desire to be experienced as
flawless, reassured and reflected

to capture, a testament of my own
desirability, the pitfall of feminine ego,
for the sake of living in the moment,
i may settle for pleasure.

vice of all vices, love of lovers,
seeker of perfection, giver of life,
let me lay down my vanity
for the rawness of gratification.

2. a favor

limitations of physical form
taking turns
patience
practice
confronting desire
depth
differences
and i describe in words
what i want in action
because i want to feel the room spin

3. the game

attention as otherworldly
as the passage of time,
commanding thoughts,
actions, and desires
deliberately stirs interest
in others. to want for nothing
is to have everything,
to give kindness is to have
kindness, and if you want to
leave their jaws on the floor-
know yourself before anyone else can.

the game of seduction lies in the direction of attention

4. fated

i kept you there at arms length
a comfortable distance
there when i needed you
unready to love you
and we weren't destined
to be husband and wife
only an eventual lovership
i had to be cautious
and test you with simple tasks
only to observe you
lusting for tenderness

5. woman

i want to be the kaleidoscope of women
i loved when I watched them.
does that make me a heroine?
yes, and it's true we have a love story on our hands.

snakes peered from behind the glass eyeballs
of men who had cheated. he preferred a different
protagonist.
one with longer eyelashes and a fatter stomach.
she was more agreeable at the time,

but she is still every woman on the inside.
the woman who saw the first woman on the
black and white television and fell in love.
what was it about her?

with a silver bowl of a pit in her stomach.
a wife? a mother? an actress? did it matter? an angel?
the unattainable void left cold silence in the air.
she was green eyed and brunette and maybe

she was just every woman yearning for
what every other woman had that made them happy.
yes, she is jealous. yes, she is lonely. that won't that stop

her

from morphing more and more into the woman on the television screen.

6. artist

it was in the same way a sculptor manipulated clay,
caressing was how it always seemed to start.
an imprint on the skin, as if to remind my wooer,
you are water
not a project to be finished or a deadline to be met
i will make you mud and you will become your body
together we will create something visionary

7. october

dark red
brush strokes
rouge and thigh highs
to keep warm
harsh romantic urges
the underbelly of a
monogamous
consuming
partnership.
to love was to
posses.

to posses was
to consume fully
or spit out a pure
love, flawed.
the sweetest
thing turned bitter
to give from the heart
and receiving
conditionally.
the cup empties,
eventually.

8. i love you

i love you
indicates familiarity
i love you
indicates emotional ties
i love you
can be euphoric
i love you
devastating
i love you
coercive
i love you
solidifying

"i love you"

i
don't
know
what
that
means

9. held

a guilty pleasure of a midnight
craving. touch starved my body
imagines being grazed lightly
feathers across my skin

running into the ocean off the
sandy beaches in maine to
dip my fingers slightly, placing
saltwater on my lips. my mind
wanders to a loving embrace.

but to be held. truly held. in all
of my emotionalism. unconditionally.
crushed by the thought that weighs on
my heart heavy. heaving and sobbing.
my stomach churns. only I could stir
these emotions in me.

*why fall in love, outsource my heart breaking, when I
can do it all by myself?*

10. tragedy

mesmerized by lips
spoken into seduction
illusive hedonistic fulfillment
followed by
repeated
denial

when the end is not guaranteed
next moves unpredictability
craving what hasn't yet
been shown
tasted
grasped

a tragedy of human nature, to want what we can't have

11. the sensualist

to enjoy one's own body
an act of rebellion
against all of those who wish
to impose their pleasures

12. vitality

youth kept us in the age of endless experiments
to be vital was to be precious, loved, protected
we rose with the sun in those days
the hum of the cicadas
water falls fell and the stars all had their turn at
the high point in the sky over the fields
where we would find lightening bugs and dragon flies

the memory serves to remind us of natural elements

13. lancelot

he said he needed a woman of virtue.
chaste, never giving in.
he longed to be the exception.

she said she needed a man of valor.
a knight of the round table.
integrity became him.

14. feel

the pleasure one prefers will multiply
and there lies the truth of abundance.

one thought of him became many.
the infatuation kept me drunk.

i considered every time a thought crept up
as taboo as longing for impossible things.

every thought, I'd visualize, wishes can come true.
every prayer, every heartbeat, a pleasure to have met
you.

15. the mind's eye

may my mind align with yours
in its eye we may meet each other.
a true melding intellectually.
it was never skin deep.

16. femme

feminine is set apart by her masculine qualities.
her ability to get ahead, annihilate the competition,

the archetypal feminine strength, the ability to be self
reliant
to provide, protect, and maintain femininity in a mans
world.

the great mother, always fruitful, bestowing her
blessings,
portal between seen and unseen, a steadfast quality.

maiden, seeking safety, unsure yet of the connection to
her own
divinity. innocence and loss thereof. rises from ash in the
wake of defeat.

crone, the final act of becoming who she was all along. a
return
to innocence accompanied by the wisdom she sought out
all her life.

17. masc

he was nurturing and kind
firm with determined
a perfect balance of
egoic pride and humility
leader, reasoner, thinker

a divine woman seeks a philosopher king

18. limb to limb

the arms of the giving tree,

branches of love offerings.

here, take the body I have

carried all my life. i trust,

limb to limb, a repeated

giving in. you'll find and

take what love you can

and through my memory

i am brought back to life.

19. eros

a wave of fire
emotionality
receiving you

bending as
water does
allowing life

fallible and
unwavering
as it can be

to be gentle
at once in
my body

www.ingramcontent.com/pod-product-compliance
Lightning Source LLC
Chambersburg PA
CBHW071247140726
47996CB00007B/2788